I AM PRETTY

By
Sonia A. Adams

Copyright © 2020 by Sonia Adams

I Am Pretty
by Sonia A. Adams

Printed in the United States of America

All rights reserved solely by the author. The author guarantees all contents are original and do not infringe upon the legal rights of any other person or work. No part of this publication may be reproduced, stored in retrieval system, or transmitted, in any form or by any means, electronic, mechanical, photocopying, recorder or otherwise without prior permission of the Author.

Unless otherwise indicated, Scripture is taken from the Holy Bible, the King James Version (KJV) or New King James Version (NKJV), copyright © 1982 by Thomas Nelson, Inc.

If you decide to host a book club, books and a facilitator's guide can be purchased at: www.soniaadams.com or go to iampretty.us

For speaking engagements or to have the author come and share with a group, please fill out the contact information on Sonia's website. www.soniaadams.com

Also, if you desire to purchase any I Am Pretty T-shirts, tanks, sweatshirts, and/or bags. All the "I Am Pretty" products are also on the website.

Contact and Social Media sites:
www.soniaadams.com
Email: soniasiampretty@gmail.com
Facebook: Sonia Adams
Instagram: soniaaadams
Twitter: @SoniaAAdams

ABOUT THE AUTHOR

Sonia is an inspirational speaker because she inspires others by sharing biblical principles that provoke purpose and helps draw people closer to God. She gives unique insight and a relevant perspective to her speaking and writing. Her wisdom crushes the barriers that keep women from receiving physical, mental, and spiritual healing. An encounter from her preaching awakens a fire and passion which causes women to pursue and fully walk in their purpose. People are waiting on Sonia and problems need her solutions. It's through her journey, trials, process, and tears she has come to a resolve to be authentically herself. She is very transparent and real about growing into womanhood and the challenges of being a female but reveals how she became a tenacious and triumphant woman who has risen to tell her story and empower women.

She is the founder and CEO of Blossoming Vines Ministries, Inc. a non-profit 501c3 whose mission is "Helping women 'Blossom' in their lives and extend their reach to others!" Her organization helps single moms and mentors elementary and high school girls. You can learn more about Blossoming Vines (www.blossomingvines.com)

In the spring of 2005, Sonia published her first book now called I Am Ready (ready for purpose, ready to be better, and ready to love) which identifies the major desires that all women (of all cultures) have- desiring love, happiness, and purpose. Her second booklet entitled Only A Little Distance To Success was self-published in November of 2010 and deals with letting go of the past to catch hold of your future. I Am Pretty is the second book in her I Am Series and I Am Married will be released in the fall of 2020.

She is a high school graduate of Griffin High. She continued to receive her BS Degree in Language Arts Education from Tuskegee University while earning a Master's Degree with honors from Oral Roberts University.

Sonia is married to Mr. Shawn Michael Adams of Dallas, Texas, who is Dean of Students at Atlanta Technical College. They reside in Atlanta, Georgia with their sons, Solomon and Simeon Michael Adams, who are the joys of her life.

May the
Lord bless
you
All that He
has for you
will come to
pass

Walk in your
Pretty
for a dime

Acknowledgements

I am grateful to God, my rock, my foundation, and His Spirit gives me strength and guidance in all things. Without Him, I am nothing.

I also desire to thank Shawn Adams, my loving husband, who encourages me to fulfill my dreams and complete everything that God placed on the inside of me. His love is deep and remains constant. I can't wait to see what the next twenty-five years hold.

Chester and Shirley Milner gave me life and continue to be my biggest cheerleaders in every stage of my journey. Robby and Jerry, we are blessed to call them mom and dad, and I am blessed to call you brothers and Sabrina my sister. My Milner (Reuben and Anna) and Smith (Andrew and Lizzie) family is strong and the lineage from whom I come.

My BFF, Sonny Hill, you get me. You inspire me and see greatness in me even when I doubt. Thank you for understanding that purpose is more than a pretty face and seeing depth in me beyond the physical.

Stephanie, Tanjala, and Tonya—our bond is tight and resilient. We support each other, pray together, and encourage each other to shine. Stephanie- you are a rock. Tanjala—you're one of the sweetest persons I know. Tonya—your triumphant spirit has always been an example for me.

To my other sister friends— we are a strong village. You know who you are! Because of my village—I am Pretty (Purposed, Received, Earmarked, Tenacious, Triumphant, and Yielded). Without you, I would not be who I am! Thanks for allowing your pretty pictures to adorn the cover. To all my sisters, near and far, I love you all!

My spiritual mentors, mamas, and pastor/teachers—thank you! Co-pastor Sylvia, Mom Charletta Benjamin, Prophetess Pam Vinnett, Pastor Shawn Adams, and Pastor Jeremy Tuck—I hope I make you proud!

Solomon and Simeon, I acknowledge you last but not least. Words cannot adequately describe the love I have for both of you. Your birth days brought great joy and you have taught me unconditional love. You are the reasons why I live and I pray my example and life will make an indelible impact on both of you forever and will reverberate for generations to come.

I AM PRETTY
By Sonia A. Adams

Purposed
Received
Earmarked
Tenacious
Triumphant
Yielded

TABLE OF CONTENTS

INTRODUCTION 9

CHAPTER 1
Purposed – *When you know and understand what you were born to accomplish in the earth.* 12

CHAPTER 2
Received – *Accepted by Him, apart from what any other human thinks or says.* 23

CHAPTER 3
Earmarked – *God has handpicked me and designated me for a specific purpose* 34

CHAPTER 4
Tenacious – *A woman with a tenacious spirit is determined, persists in life, and rises above her challenges.* 42

CHAPTER 5
Triumphant – *Achieving an exciting life full of victory and success.* 51

CHAPTER 6
Yielded – *Emphasizes yielding as a twofold concept which includes yielding to the Father so that we can yield more fruit.* 60

FINAL THOUGHTS 73

INTRODUCTION

As women, we are bombarded by the expectation to appear and act picture perfect most of the time. Often women are judged by our exterior and ability to look aesthetically appealing and carry ourselves in a way that attracts others into our space. Sometimes opportunities present themselves to professional women who are well kept. And this causes the need for cosmetics, hair salons, plastic surgeons, and a booming fashion industry – women are their greatest customers. We find ourselves in the vicious cycle to maintain award winning appearances! Outer looks become the focus and goal, so we spend time, money, and energy to achieve this goal!

If you can look at yourself in the mirror and say "I am Pretty," it likely stems from you making an unfair perception based on external attributes! If you see your flaws, imperfections, and wrinkles, you may think "I am not Pretty." Again, you are viewing your outer shell and making an unfair evaluation of who you are based upon your outer appearance.

You may look in the mirror and see a beautiful face, pleasant skin tone, and a banging figure. You have learned to love your curves, your laugh lines, your freckles and all of you and can say, "I am Pretty"! Though your confession is resolute, again it only affirms that which is external! **Relying on acceptance based on physical attributes inhibits our ability to see, know, and understand who we really are.**

This is why there's a need for continuous affirmation and approval from others! When our confidence, esteem and the foundation of our self-worth is built on the outer appearance, it's shaky and requires continual praise, affirmation, and stroking! This is why Facebook and Instagram have become the cornerstone of our culture! They are the devices that strokes our ego, affirms our confidence, and assures our pretty.

Unfortunately, if we're not careful, we'll need "**likes and loves**" daily in order to feel good about who we are. External qualities become the deciding factor upon which we base our approval, first by us and then by others! They breed comparison, wield jealousy, and foster discontentment. These feelings of insecurity arise in us, because maybe we don't know how powerful and remarkable we really are.

Who are we in our created soul, apart from our physical shell? Who are we apart from what we do, and what we've accomplished?

When we don't know who we are as created spiritual beings and can't fully answer these questions, it is likely that we have not had a radical inner change that is solidified and sealed in us. Until this earnestly happens within us, **we will never truly believe we are pretty or that we are enough.**

I came to this revelation because, though I felt pretty on the outside and people told me I was beautiful, I was still insecure and unsure of who I was as a mighty creation of God. I didn't know who I was as an approved woman who was precious apart from my looks, my titles, and what I did. I never felt good enough, smart enough, thin enough, worthy enough, or ironically, pretty enough.

Pretty can become a word that we say to young girls who wear pretty ruffled dresses, ponytails with cute bows and smiles on cue! Pretty is what we say when a face is beat and lashes are on fleek! Pretty is the thought I have when my dress is tapered, and my high heels give me a strut that make men nearly start drooling as they look.

Pretty was a word that had no value or depth for me until it came to life, after I discovered an acrostic that gave it real meaning! I uncovered that pretty is a girl, a teenager or a woman who has a purpose, and is received, earmarked, tenacious, triumphant and yielded!

When a woman finds herself embracing these aspects of PRETTY (*purpose, received, earmarked, tenacious, triumphant, and yielded*) and they become deeply rooted on the inside, her pretty aroma will become her foundation, stability and strength! Once we blossom in our pretty, we can extend our reach to others. And these principles will become a source of freedom to many other women who are stuck in their outer pretty!

This acrostic is explored in this book in six concise chapters containing principles laced with God's wisdom to help you discover the keys to unlock things within you. This will help give you a solid sense of identity, purpose, and victory in your life. Journey with me through these pages and let's take a deeper look at the meaning of *PRETTY* [purposed, received, earmarked, tenacious, triumphant, and yielded] and watch God ignite a deep work in the core of your being that will give you the godly confidence and assurance to do and become all He has purposed you to be, do and walk, in your PRETTY!

CHAPTER 1

*P*urposed

Years ago, Rick Warren wrote a book entitled *The Purpose Driven Life*, which spoke to humankind about our need and desire for a life with purpose. Obviously, this is an astounding truth, because God created us for a purpose, and life without purpose is vain and fruitless.

"What is my purpose?" This was a thought that pierced my mind and heart as a teenage girl. I always felt there was more to life than having a pretty face and the ability to play sports. Because my life was void of purpose, I stood tall on the fact that I had a pretty smile, a nice figure, and a winning shot in basketball. This was the foundation of my confidence and the core of who I was, and I constantly needed others to affirm these attributes for me to feel good about myself.

I went out of my way to make sure I was seen by wearing revealing clothes, having my face beat and my hair laid. With basketball, I set out to score the most points and be the best player on my team. I lived for the applause of men and I did everything in my power to get it. It made me feel important and valuable, but inside I felt like a trophy with no depth, no purpose, and no real intention for living my life. My goals were selfish and grounded in my need for continual accolades and applause which never led to an inner assurance that was strong and sure. My esteem was built on my physical attributes and not from the core of who I was.

Like me, maybe your confidence stems from your beautiful face, voluptuous thighs, gorgeous smile, or perfect figure. Or maybe it's not in your pretty face or your athletic ability, but in your phenomenal voice, artistic ability, or dance prowess. Maybe your confidence is in your uncanny intelligence, family notoriety, or wealth. Or is it your great speaking ability, leadership, successful career or another trait that affirms your confidence and defines your value and worth.

I'm sure you know the trait that gives you pride and is your trump card. You know you're great in this area and everybody else knows it too. Or maybe you find yourself on the total opposite side of this spectrum, because you don't feel you have any foundation to stand on. You don't feel that you are pretty, or have any qualities that give you worth, value, or purpose.

You may feel useless, ugly, dumb, inadequate, unlovable, and void of a reason for your existence, but know that God sees value and worth in you, despite what you may feel. No matter what side of the spectrum you find yourself, it is not who you truly are. Our superficial thoughts about ourselves are based on that which is temporal and **not the full truth of who we really are**.

God's purpose for us goes far beyond our appearance and abilities. He sees in us what we cannot see in ourselves. He desires for us to understand **how and why we were created.** We must move beyond our thoughts about ourselves and reach towards His thoughts about us and His plan and purpose for us.

God's thoughts toward us are so wonderful and positive. As you read the positive and affirming words below that the Father speaks about you, they can begin to transform any shallow thoughts you have about yourself, and help you internalize what God sees and says about you.

Psalms 139:13-18 in the New Living Translation says:

> You made all the delicate, inner parts of my body and knit me together in my mother's womb. Thank you for making me so wonderfully complex! Your workmanship is marvelous—how well I

know it. You watched me as I was being formed in utter seclusion, as I was woven together in the dark of the womb. You saw me before I was born. Every day of my life was recorded in your book. Every moment was laid out before a single day had passed. How precious are your thoughts about me, O God. They cannot be numbered! I can't even count them; they outnumber the grains of sand! And when I wake up, you are still with me!"

Psalm 139:14 says, "I will praise thee; for I am fearfully and wonderfully made: marvelous are thy works; and that my soul knoweth right well." (NKJV)

1 Peter 2:9 tells us, "But ye are a chosen generation, a royal priesthood, a holy nation, a peculiar people; that ye should shew forth the praises of him who hath called you out of darkness into his marvellous light . . ." (NKJV)

Song of Solomon 1:5 says Behold, thou art fair, my love; Behold thou art fair; Thine eyes are [as] doves." (NKJV)

Ephesians 2:10 NKJV says, "For we are His workmanship, created in Christ Jesus for good works, which God prepared beforehand that we should walk in them."

Gen 1:26 says, "Then God said, 'Let Us make man in Our image, according to Our likeness; let them have dominion over the fish of the sea, over the birds of the air, and over the cattle, over all the earth and over every creeping thing that creeps on the earth'." (NKJV)

These Scriptures tell us that we are fearfully and wonderfully made, chosen, royal, fair (pleasant), His workmanship (poem), created for good works, and made in His awesome image and likeness. When you meditate on these reminders of what God says about you, you can reaffirm yourself daily. Speak daily that you are fearfully and wonderfully made, royal, unique, and made in His image and likeness. Remember you are His workmanship created for good works.

Yes, you are royal, a detailed work, and tapestry of the Creator and He took His time and specifically fashioned you with intricacy and precision. He created us in His image and likeness. Not only did He create us, but **He made us for a purpose** – for good works in the earth. So I am not just royal and fabulous, but my awesomeness has purpose. When I walk in purpose, the more my **inner pretty** permeates the atmosphere, which causes a change in me and extends to others.

You too may ask, "What is my purpose?" Purpose can be vague and hard to figure out. I love the following quotes from the late Dr. Myles Munroe:

> **Purpose is when you know and understand what you were born to accomplish.** Vision is when you see it in your mind and begin to imagine it. The purpose of a thing is the original intent or desire of the one who created it. The manufacturer determines both the products purpose and how it will function to fulfill that purpose [1]

Therefore, to discover our purpose, we must garner an intimate relationship with God, who is our Creator and Manufacturer. An intimate relationship with God means having an encounter with

God for real. In this encounter, ask God to touch your heart, change your unhealthy perceptions of yourself, and receive His love.

He alone knows **the original reason He created you**, **what you were born to accomplish**, and **how you will function to fulfill it**. And His desire is to reveal it to you with clarity and for you to allow Him to guide you in how to fulfill it.

It is not a one-time revelation, but an ongoing relationship with the Father who leads and guides us on a purposeful life journey that will have ebbs and flows, ups and downs, but has a victorious expected end. Therefore, we must start the journey and keep going until the end, completing all that God has purposed us to do.

When we fail to unlock the reality of our purpose, we tend to feel lifeless, depressed, stressed, and just go through the motions. Or unfortunately, we may find that we need something external such as drugs, alcohol, people – anything to dull our thoughts just to live through another day.

Before I discovered my purpose, the external fix I needed was not drugs or alcohol, but constant validation from others and the need to be loved by a man, even if that man treated me like dung. Therefore, I did things to assure that I got both love and validation. I found myself always trying to please people, doing things for others even if it cost me my dignity, self-worth, and time.

Thus, I desired to literally go to Hollywood, pursue a career in modeling, live a glamorous life so others would see and validate me. Men would complement my pretty and others would applaud my success. And when it came to men and relationships, I found myself lowering my standards and crawling into the beds of various men, because I believed if I snagged the right one, he would give me purpose and make me feel loved and wanted.

Unfortunately, I was used sexually, abused verbally, and never found a meaningful relationship that gave me the love and purpose I desired. In fact, no man or person can give us purpose. We are all imperfect beings and no human can ever adequately love and affirm us the way God can.

Fortunately, I was twenty-two years old when I realized God had created me for far more than just being a pretty face, someone's booty call, and a people pleaser. When I fully surrendered my life to God, I realized I was created for more, and that my life really mattered. And God desired to use me for something much greater and more meaningful than the selfish ambitious, and meaningless aspirations I'd dreamt for myself.

He had fashioned me first to love Him, and as He loves me back, His love picked me up and gave me purpose and joy. He told me I was to be His mouthpiece in the earth, a carrier of good deeds, and a stirrer of purpose in others. He revealed that I'm a wife, a mother to many (biological and spiritual), a mentor to some, and conduit of change that advocates for the least of these.

He created me to speak when others will not speak, to rattle and challenge systems, and reach my hand – with His power – to those places where His light is dim and His love in unknown. He created me to write, and to help others unlock their dreams and overcome their past. I am made to speak healing and freedom, and to assist others in finding their purpose.

This full clarity of my purpose was not completely understood at twenty-two years of age, but God gave me enough insight that I began to prepare myself to become everything He created me to be and to do everything He purposed me to do.

His Word was my instruction, His voice my guide, and my steps of faith are leading me to walk in the right direction. It's not always easy. In fact, there have been times I desired to quit. Other times, I was mad at God. There were even times when what I envisioned plummeted and I felt despair, felt unsuccessful, and did not quite understand why life was taking me in an unfamiliar direction.

In the midst of walking in purpose, understand that everything will not be peaches and cream. You and I will suffer heartache and pain, loss and disappointments, rejection, and we won't get everything in this life that we want. However, to find your God-given purpose and fulfill it is the greatest joy you can achieve, despite the challenges.

It renders the greatest rewards. The rewards far outweigh the negatives. The **reward is knowing I'm doing exactly what God has purposed me to do** and touching the lives God connects me too, because I am yielded to Him and doing His will in the earth. As I walk in my created purpose, I must continue to do exactly what I was born to do.

I fulfill this in whatever door He opens and whatever place He sends me. I extend my love towards Him and He reciprocates and allows me to share His love first to my family, friends, spiritual family, and to others here and around the world. My purpose is the P in my PRETTY and I will continue to fulfill His will as long as I have breath and He gives me the strength to do so. This is my joy and it fuels my passion.

Likewise, when God reveals your purpose and you get a glimpse and understanding of why you were created and what you are purposed to do in the earth, true joy and fulfillment will fill your heart and fuel your passion for life. Again, the journey will take turns, ups and downs, and even detours, but you have to continue to ask God for directions and instructions with every step you take. **Each of us has unique talents and gifts that were placed inside of us that are specifically connected to what we were created to do**. Each of us has been given an assignment to make a difference in this world in such a way that lives are changed, systems are shaken, and souls are reached for an earthly and eternal existence!

Pause and ask yourself, who am I, apart from that thing I'm most confident in? Do I feel not so pretty or unworthy? Who am I and do I have a purpose? Let's take a moment to answer these questions. First, you answer them and then let's discover what God's Word says about these and see if you know and understand your purpose and are able to continue or start taking steps toward the destined reason why you were born and put in the earth at this time and in this place.

[1] Munroe, Myles. *Purpose for Living*. Shippensburg: Destiny Image, Inc., 2011.

Journal Entry #1

1. What is that area that I feel most confident in? Why?

   _____
   _____
   _____
   _____

2. Who am I apart from that area that I am confident?

   _____
   _____
   _____
   _____

3. What areas do I condemn myself and why? Do I lack confidence?

   _____
   _____
   _____
   _____

4. Who am I and do I have a purpose

   _____
   _____
   _____
   _____

5. What is my purpose?

   _____
   _____
   _____
   _____

After answering the questions, it is important to note that purpose becomes clear as we continually seek God and He gives us instructions. We must walk out those instructions as we get them and understand them.

> Habakkuk 2:2-3 tells us, "Then the LORD answered me and said: **"Write the vision and make [it] plain on tablets**, That he may run who reads it. For the vision [is] yet for an appointed time; But at the end it will speak, and it will not lie. Though it tarries, wait for it; Because it will surely come, It will not tarry." (KJV)

We must write our vision down so we can see it and know there's a process to it being fully realized, but as we move in God's will, it will surely come to pass.

I would suggest that you write your overall vision and then write out the specifics that you're asked to walk out daily, weekly, monthly, and yearly. Often, we get ideas or get excited about what we're going to do, but we fail to get a strategic plan of action to carry it out. Or we create our plans and try to force them to happen.

In order to get divine strategy, we must seek God and hear His purposed plan. In addition to praying and getting His will, we can utilize life coaches, business consultants, or experts in the areas we are pursuing. It is also helpful to get training that will be helpful in accomplishing our vision and purpose.

I encourage Godly wisdom, counsel, training, and coaching and I've used all of these tools while pursuing purpose. I will end this chapter by giving you an example of my purpose written as a general vision statement and then share a couple of specific instructions God gave me as I continue to walk in my purpose.

My vision is to be a conduit/mouthpiece and servant of God who provokes purpose in others and brings them closer to God by educating and communicating His Word to bring physical, mental, and spiritual healing. Also, my purpose is to help men and women become free, and surrender to God. This year my specific instructions include:

1. Spend intimate time with the Father daily to hear from Him and get strength and directives for the journey.
2. To complete this book and tasks given to me as a pastor and to be ready to speak His Word, and share His love in every open door He shows me, whether in the United States or abroad.
3. To finish my business plan and all that is involved in that process and launch the product for sale.

These are just three specific statements of instruction from God, but God speaks and opens doors along the path so you and I can continue to walk out our purpose. Jesus says it best in John 14:32, **"But I will do what the Father requires of me,** so that the world will know that I love the Father" (NLT).

Let's start progressing in our purpose. Your purpose will be fulfilled as you do what the Father requires of you. Be open and ready as He shows you, leads you, and requires you to serve and do things for Him as He requests. What **He requires** is **your ability to hear**, **availability to do and go**, and **willingness to say yes**, no matter the costs.

Yes, it will take faith, letting go of your fears, being bold, understanding how your gifts, talents, and profession all work in concert, and it will take a surrendering of your will. Most importantly, our desire to do all that God requires of us should be the ultimate desire above all things. You are not just a pretty shell, but you are a purpose driven woman who pleases the Father and shares His love so that others, too, can experience freedom and also walk in their pretty **purpose!**

CHAPTER 2

Received

To start this chapter, I will simply define "received" as **acceptance from someone that has an important and highly influential role in your life**. Being received as worthy by someone we love is likely one of the most important experiences that we can encounter. When we receive this kind of love and affirmation, especially from God, it gives us full confidence and freedom in our lives.

Fully grasping and organically ascertaining the truth that God receives us despite our imperfections, flaws, and our daily missing the mark can by-pass us if we do not intentionally allow it to be established in our heart. **<u>We are received and accepted by God regardless of what we think about ourselves and despite what any other human thinks or says about us.</u>**

Acceptance helps us feel that our life is valuable and worthy of existence. Healthy affirmation can guide the very core of our being. **Every human soul, whether they admit it or not, desires to be affirmed and acknowledged as important, needed, purposeful, and loved!**

Empires have fought to earn it! Kings have striven to gain it! Queens have loved to receive it! Princes have hoped to inherit it and princesses have longed to behold it. Women lose themselves to earn it and men excel to find it! In every accomplishment, dream, and purpose under the sun, we all desire to hear, "**<u>You are important</u>, <u>you have value</u>, and <u>your life matters</u>!**"

Many times, people can diminish our worth and make us feel less than worthy. As a result, we may attempt to find affirmation and approval in numerous unhealthy ways. I can relate to trying to find acceptance from others. As I shared in Chapter 1, when I was not received or validated by others, I did whatever it took to get their approval and acceptance, even if I lost my dignity and compromised my character to gain it.

I don't know the time or that place where lack of love and affirmation left you feeling empty, void of purpose, or trying to prove something to yourself and others to quiet the voices in your mind and those who said, "You could not, would not, never would be," and never affirmed you.

But you know that place that left a hole in your heart, though it may be a painful to remember. You probably can name the time and place where God's love and receipt was stolen from you or ruined within you. If you would be honest, this place still hurts, causes you doubt and frustration at times, and has caused a lack of confidence in who you really are.

The void caused by not being received and affirmed is the paramount reason why so many people need and desire external sources to stroke our egos and affirm our being. We do everything in our power, either knowingly or unknowingly, to get it. We count the number of likes on Facebook and Instagram. We post pictures of ourselves daily to get affirmation and approval. In fact, social media is an instant gratifier that causes people to create fake images, false narratives, and filtered lives all to get the approval of people who don't really know us.

We crave validation, acceptance, likes, and loves. Being received is more than instant gratification; it should be an innate part of who we are. God put the desire to be loved and affirmed inside all of us! However, His desire is for us to fully receive it from Him first, which is the foundation of our being and the pillar that launches us into strength, power, and assurance! **His love and affirmation is a deep work in the soul (the mind, heart, and spirit) that God alone can accomplish.**

Even as I am writing the chapters of this book, though I dedicated my life to God at twenty-two years of age, I am just now beginning to allow this poignant truth to seep deep into my spirit and change the very core of my thinking and the depths of my being. Now more than ever, I am beginning to see myself beyond a pretty face, my career success, and my ministry achievements. I'm fully grasping that no matter how I look (which is fading and subjective), what I do, or what I accomplish – God has already received me because **He created me and accepted me just as I am**.

So you and I no longer have to do, look, or try to achieve great feats to be accepted by God. He already accepts us and all He desires is that we love and receive Him so that His love, freedom, and healing can free us. We must discover that we are received by God and believe what He believes and says about us.

If we don't see ourselves whole and affirmed by Him, it can lead to a difficult journey of striving to produce a false image that many times doesn't match what we truly believe about ourselves. Discovering **The Father's** affirmation and it becoming a reality in your heart is the only way you can overcome that place in your life where you were rejected, lied to, and hurt. This discovery doesn't happen overnight, and it is a process of being honest, vulnerable, and being able to visit that place where affirmation was stripped from you. You have to begin to ask God to heal that broken place and mend your broken heart. Then you can receive His acceptance and walk in assurance as it permeates your being and organically flows from your person.

I can recall two places where my self-worth was ripped from me and caused my identity to be fractured and my self-worth to be flawed. First, I'll share a subtle, not-so-violent way my esteem was lost. It started when I was a little girl. I could remember adults, church members, and others saying, "She's such a pretty little girl. Oh, isn't she adorable?"

As I grew, these flatteries continued to follow me and I'd hear people say, "she's cute," or "she thinks she's cute." And sometimes, people would say, "She's light, bright, and d@%# near white." Boys would say, "Girl you're fine. Oh, your legs are shapely and your butt voluptuous and I like what I see."

Over the years, this began to give me a complex. I truly began to believe I was nothing more than an empty shell and a piece of meat. A girl with nothing more to offer than a lovely smile and some nice skin. Nevertheless, it gained me attention and the more attention I got, the more I fed it.

That space from kindergarten to college produced a mindset where **I reduced my self-worth and identity to thick thighs, a six-pack, a big, curvy butt, and a lovely smile**. I didn't feel received or loved unless those words were spoken to me, and ironically, I needed those words of affirmation to feel good about myself, which was always temporary.

Additionally, because my value and purpose were based solely on my appearance, I too valued others based upon their appearance. If they looked a certain way, I judged them to act or be a certain way and sized them up based on appearance alone. The same measure I judged, approved, and disapproved myself was the same measure of judgment I extended towards others. What flawed thinking and what an unbalanced person was I?

Fortunately, it took God's power to begin to dismantle this lie, help me discover His truth, and begin to understand my self-worth was not in my exterior, but that He receives me because of who I am! God loves the "me" He created and He helped me to love and value all people and see that we are all valuable to God. My mind was renewed and my flawed thinking changed.

However, there was a second place in my life that caused my self-worth to hit rock bottom before I changed. It was the nail in the coffin. It was the day someone spoke disheartening and rejecting words to me at a tender age when I was eager, full of excitement and zeal, and ready to conquer the world. I ran to this person that I esteemed highly and shared with them a dream I had for my life. They told me I could never fulfill my dream because women aren't equipped to do what I dreamt. I was told as long as I aspired to fulfill this dream, everything I touched would fail.

It was that place in my life that lack of affirmation from a person I admired caused my identity to depreciate even more. Both feeling like a pretty, empty shell and the absence of approval and encouragement from an important person in my life left me utterly defeated, which spiraled into a twenty-four-year journey to find value, worth, and confidence for real.

This is my story and the places in my life that snatched my identity and caused me to feel devalued. Nobody knows your story, nor the place(s) where affirmation was stripped from you and how it has shattered and caused you great pain, desperation, and failure over the course of your life.

I'd like to share another story where affirmation was stolen from a young lady whose identity will remain anonymous. Her honor and value were taken from her in a brutal, gruesome, and violent way. She was young, innocent, and pretty and happened to be at a party with friends. On this particular night, she slipped into a room with a young boy she liked. The boy summoned quite a few other boys to come and join the fun, as he saw it. As a result, she was raped and violated, not only by one male, but by a handful of boys, over and over again. She was the victim of a gang rape and left that party that night fractured, physically and mentally hurt, suicidal, and totally humiliated. She would spend the rest of her life trying to overcome this despicable act that left her empty, void of purpose and un-received.

The pain of this detestable act causes tears to swell in my eyes even now and you may also feel the heaviness of this terrible tragedy! Whether you had a horrific, detestable act done to you, or you failed to have someone speak affirmation into your life, the fact remains that negative events have happened to you and it has infected your self-worth and identity. Therefore, you must: 1. **acknowledge what happened**, 2. **identify the place where it happened**, 3. **forgive the person or people**, 4. **heal the wound it caused**, 5. **begin**

the process to overcome it, and 6. **finish the process to rise above it**.

I hope that hearing my story and hers will cause you to identify the place where lack of affirmation was absent or stripped from you. This can start the process of healing and freedom for you. We live in a fallen world with fallen, imperfect, and even some wicked humans. Some of our stories are gut wrenching, while others are not as horrific, but we all have a story that has caused pain and affected our identity and purpose.

Lack of affirmation not only causes pain, but unhealthy behavior, anger, cowardice, and a host of other issues that we must journey to overcome to become the person God desires for us to be. Our identity can be skewed, our mind altered, and our confidence shattered by our past and every day can be a struggle to wake up, believe in ourselves, believe in others, and even believe in a God who can take the pain away and make us whole.

Over time, as we endeavor to trust God, we can find complete healing and the ability to live a rewarding and successful life. But only God the Father is able to miraculously heal you or any person who experiences something tragic or painful. He can help us find the power to forgive which is also necessary for us to be whole. When this process of healing happens, it will bring the affirmation, honor, and worth to excel in our designed purpose.

This is why an earthly father's affirmation has the potential to add value to our lives, if it is extended in a healthy way. Even more significantly, the receipt of the Heavenly Father's affirmation exceeds all human approval, value, and encouragement. He has the omniscient power and unconditional love to overshadow the deficits of human beings.

This process of healing will not happen overnight. It is a journey of believing, doubting, and failure. In the journey, you'll also find success but sometimes feel paranoia while stepping forward then backwards, but continue pressing towards God and His purposes for your life. If you're willing to be honest, vulnerable, and visit that place where affirmation was **stripped from you**, or **not properly given to you and begin to receive the Heavenly Father's affirmation and journey through His process of healing, true purpose and joy is ahead!**

Undoubtedly, your life will never be the same and you will find yourself soaring and walking in the fullness of all God called you to be and do! You, like I, can unlock the door that was once a stumbling block in your life. Let's explore the journal pages to unlock some keys to healing and overcoming the places that attempted to destroy your identity and receipt from the Father.

Journal Entry #2

1. Describe an incident or time in your life where value and honor were stripped from you. What was said and done?

   _____
   _____
   _____
   _____

2. Do you desire to get healed from this and what do you think it will take to do so?

   _____
   _____
   _____
   _____

3. Are you ready to start the journey and rise above it? Why or why not?

   _____
   _____
   _____
   _____

4. Describe your relationship with God, the Heavenly Father.

   _____
   _____
   _____
   _____

5. Do you feel this relationship can become better? If so, how?

   _____
   _____
   _____
   _____

6. What does it mean for you to be received and affirmed by God? Are you? Why or why not?

_____
_____
_____
_____
_____
_____

After answering the questions in the journal pages, you may find yourself in tears, still feeling helpless and maybe ashamed, but the solutions below will be helpful in continuing in this process.

So where do you start? How do you journey through a process to see change and freedom in your life? I will share a few godly principles below, but everyone's process is unique, and God guides us in many different ways to get healed and find peace in our lives.

First, begin to talk to God and ask Him to heal that place that scarred you. Ask Him to take away the pain and give you the supernatural ability to forgive. Or begin to play worship music and sit in His presence while He calms your heart and allow a complete healing process.

For me, I had to find a more thorough and deeper path to healing and wholeness. I asked for prayer of deliverance from Christians who understood the power of prayer and were able to reject evil spirits that had attached themselves to my heart and mind. This kind of prayer is not always popular, and some don't believe in praying against evil forces, but sometimes, this may be the cause of our pain and unrest. So getting prayer with balanced, wise, and skillful people can be a positive path.

Also, I sought out Christian therapy to talk about the things that happened to me that destroyed my confidence and self-worth. Godly counsel helps to put at bay those past hurts and pain that become barriers in our life. Seek godly counsel and ask God to help you find people who can help you talk and walk through your healing.

Avoid comparing yourself to others you admire or see on social media, and limit your time on social media so you won't get entangled in feeling less than and not owning your self-worth.

Connect with godly friends that speak life into you and affirm who you are. **We need people in our lives who see in us what we don't see in ourselves**. They see our pretty inside and out and they encourage us to be all God desires for us to be. They know how to pray and when to pray. They will not allow you to remain comfortable in mediocrity and will push you to achieve greatness. Ask God to send these type of sisters and friends into your life and believe that He will, if you don't already have these type of sister friends.

Try to read the Word consistently and learn to pray, meditate, and journal so His word can cleanse and fuel you at the same time.

Finally, as an act of positive confession, speak your confessions out loud. Post the Scriptures below somewhere in your house or some place that you're able to meditate on them and absorb them into your heart. Read the Scriptures and the paraphrased versions that I personally rewrote for you and I.

I will praise You, for I am fearfully and wonderfully made; Marvelous are Your works, And that my soul knows very well. Psalm 139:14

I was created by God with precision and I celebrate Him for making me so well!

For by grace I have been saved through faith . . . For I am His workmanship, created in Christ Jesus for good works, which God prepared beforehand that I should walk in them. Eph 2: 8-10

I am His poem and good works will follow me all the days of my life!

But I am a chosen generation, a royal priesthood, a holy nation, His own special person, that I may proclaim the praises of Him who called me out of darkness into His marvelous light; 1 Peter 2:9

Royalty is in my bloodline and I am a special, chosen person who brings light where it is dark.

For I am a holy to the LORD my God; the LORD my God has chosen me to be a people for Himself, a special treasure above all the peoples on the face of the earth. Deuteronomy 14:2

I am a treasure who is honored among many and chosen by God Himself!

Write these as screensavers on your laptop, put them on post-its or note cards and tape them to your mirror, or put them on your phone and speak them daily! These positive statements remind us that no human, earthly thing, or possession can fill the space that only God (the Creator of all humankind) can satisfy and validate! Know that you are received and continue your journey towards healing and wholeness and know that you are received and affirmed by the **All Knowing, All Seeing, Supreme, Awesome, Miracle Working, Omnipotent, Powerful,** and **Loving God**!

CHAPTER 3

*E*armarked

Lysa Terkeurst writes in her book, *It's Not Supposed to Be This Way*, "You are not a God who picks on me. **You are a God who has hand-picked me.** And I want to live a life that brings you glory." I love this quote because it reminds me that God hand-picked (**earmarked**) me and desires that my life bring light to others.

Earmarked means **designated for a particular purpose**, set aside, and set apart. Some synonyms include allocate, consecrate, dedicate, reserve, or save. These meanings alone are powerful, because they allude to the fact that God Himself has designated for us a particular purpose, and He has consecrated us and set us apart, saved and reserved us for greatness.

Psalm 4:3 says, "But know that the Lord has set apart for Himself him who is godly; The Lord will hear when I call to Him."

"Before I formed you in the womb I knew you, before you were born I set you apart..." Jeremiah 1:5.

"For I know the plans I have for you," declares the LORD, "plans to prosper you and not to harm you, plans to give you hope and a future, Jeremiah 29:11.

God earmarked you and knew what you were born to do while you were still being formed in your mother's womb. His plan is to give us hope and a future that is meaningful and brings us life and brings life to others. If we are earmarked for greatness and our pretty is destined to reach high heights and great depths, why do we see so much ugly and failure?

Unfortunately, though we have been chosen, forces come against us at an early age to steal and destroy the plan that God has for us. We live in a world where spiritual forces are real and permeate the atmosphere. Though this is not a theological dissertation to convince readers about the reality of demons and angels, it is important to know that evil and good spirits should not be deduced to mythology and fairy tales; they are a reality that we wake up to everyday.

Ironically, Hollywood has insight regarding this reality, because they often create movies where forces of darkness are battling forces of good. And many times, the good powers are endeavoring to overcome the dark powers. Often good is attributed to superheroes, light or protagonists and evil is assigned to antagonists, villains and darkness.

Also, we repeatedly hear in the news, in society, and in law enforcement, the terms inclusive of killer, liar, corrupt, fatal, and harmful. Have you ever wondered what is the source of these destructive and evil things that happen in the world? The source is dark spiritual forces that desire for us to fail. And it is necessary for you as a pretty, beautiful, chosen vessel of God to understand that there is a fight between good and evil forces that do not want you to be all that God desires you to be.

The more we grow in our understanding of God, the more we should grow in our depth and authority to defeat the dark forces that desire to inhibit our lives. Continue the journey with God and He will continue to equip you to defeat the opposition and give you understanding of the source of the evil forces and how to defeat them.

Better yet, He will release His power and knowledge to you **to help you overcome negative forces and walk in the fullness He earmarked for you**. My hope is that this chapter unveils a poignant truth that resides deep within you. I pray you defeat the evil forces that try to stop you and fulfill everything God **earmarked** you for and as you do that- **you will walk in full victory**.

So many people die never really understanding or fully doing what they were born to do. As women, we may also wander into unhealthy relationships, struggle with our designated purpose, and fail to discover what God really earmarked us for. Innately, women desire security and love. When we lack a sense of who we are and what we are earmarked for, we desire a man to complete us and fill the void in our lives. When we need a man to affirm us and he disappoints, we feel rejected and often settle for whatever a man will give us. We do this because we don't really know who we are, and we devalue ourselves and take what we can get. We find ourselves giving away our souls, mentally, spiritually, and sexually!

I found this was the case for me. I needed a man to validate me, so I settled and took whatever crumbs a man would offer, even if it meant not having someone who was deeply in love with me or not having a person who affirmed my vision, my purpose, and my heart. Even if he treated me poorly, caused me to become emotionally unsettled, cheated on me, and was physically or mentally abusive, I settled and stayed in too many unhealthy relationships.

Also, I gave men everything (even my chastity) in hopes that eventually, I would win their love and affection. But for some reason, I always fell short and many of those relationships sadly ended, thus creating more baggage, which I took into the next relationship. If you also struggle with not knowing what God earmarked you for and find yourself in an unhealthy relationship, desperately trying to discover true love, you may need to take a step back and allow the first two principles (**purposed and being received**) of PRETTY to permeate your spirit and become a part of your spiritual DNA.

Let purpose and being received by the Father become your first and foremost pursuit. Chase God and His purpose and come to the realization that His affirmation is more important than that of any man. Don't give yourself to a man who doesn't appreciate, respect, and treat you as the chosen woman you are. It may be time to let him go and ask God for the courage, strength, and ability to do so. It may not be easy to let it go, but no relationship is worth lingering in if it's not pushing us toward our destiny or causing us to be all that we were created to be!

Fortunately, God's love led me to His truth, and helped me find out what I was earmarked for! Discovering His truth about me helped me learn to be less dependent on a man and more dependent on Him for my identity, love, and purpose. I had to be honest with myself and honest with God.

Why didn't I believe in myself and why did I need a man so bad? These were the questions I had to answer. As I stated in an earlier chapter, my value was forged in my external, so my identity was quite shallow and faulty! Because I didn't know why I was created, I leaned toward desiring a man to give me an identity and purpose.

So I ask you, do you believe in yourself? Do you value the gift in you, and do you know your purpose and identity apart from a man? What did God earmark you for and are you walking in it? These are critical questions to answer and once these questions are totally discovered within your life's journey, you will find that you are better prepared to fulfill God's purpose!

And if marriage is a part of that purpose, it will happen as well. Strong, purpose-driven, confident women attract strong, purpose-driven, confident men. If you desire marriage, God desires you to be equally yoked with a man that shares your purpose, affirms you, and will help you realize your vision. He will be the one you can create children with and multiply resources in the earth as a godly couple, and you two will become world changers and generational blessers.

Fortunately, after so many failed and unhealthy relationships, my strong, confident purpose-driven man found me and we are still in love and fulfilling our purpose, both individually and as a couple. So don't settle for any man and allow any relationship to take precedence over fulfilling what God earmarked you for, because we will individually give an account for what we accomplish in the earth.

God earmarked and preserved women for a specific purpose and we have been uniquely formed and given a large dose of estrogen not just for procreation, but it ignites our delicate, compassionate, and nurturing nature, which is a part of God's destined plan for us.

Mary was able to carry the Divine Baby, escape from murderers and birthed Him in a stable with animals. Solomon shared his love for a Jewish handmaiden who won his love with her beauty and ability to attract him sensually. Only a woman can use love that is sweeter than honey, a fragrant smell, and eyes like doves to capture the attention of a man and cause his heart to beat in a different rhythm.

Rachael was beautiful in form and appearance and she was able to win the heart of Jacob who waited seven years to gain her hand in marriage. She was so powerful that she spoke life into Jacob and helped him birth a nation. Yes, a woman! Esther knew she was called to help her people in the era that she was born. She knew there was something about her femininity, her beauty, **her spiritual pretty**, and her ability to please the king that would be the catalyst to turn the heart of the king to relent from destroying her people and turn the tables and kill Haman instead.

No male has the physical makeup, nurturing fabric, internal and external beauty, ability to carry babies, and DNA to do the things God **earmarked** us to do. A woman was earmarked and given stamina to carry the Christ child, stand beside her husband as he built a nation, and turned the heart of king from destroying and slaughtering her people.

God knew it took a woman that He endowed with special qualities, keenness, and a PRETTY specific to a woman to accomplish these feats. This is why forces of darkness try to blind women from seeing their true identity and the true reason God earmarked us. Often, I see young girls and women confused and struggling with their designated purpose as a female. Or they choose to hide their feminine traits and parade masculine qualities contrary to their authentic self, according to God's word.

Not knowing why God earmarked us can lead us down an empty or self-willed path. Many unconsciously or ignorantly travel through life merely existing, doing what someone else desires them to do, or doing what society expects or influences them to do and be. Ironically, influencers carry this title and are paid to influence people to purchase products, accept a belief system, lifestyle, or behavior that may be different to what we were innately born to do and be. Therefore, we gravitate and do things that seem logical, plausible or reachable.

When we buy the lie that we are not pretty enough, feminine enough, smart enough, or worthy enough to do what we were chosen ***to be and do***, we find ourselves doing things that give us a temporary feeling of acceptance, worth, and sense of accomplishment. We dim our light as women and relegate ourselves to the status quo and do what is expected of us. Some women who miss the opportunity to choose may be forced to become sexual objects for men, homebodies, or fledgling in a lack-luster career. **When we do something that is not our ultimate desire, we feel unfulfilled, used, trapped, or exhausted** <u>while seeing everyone else's dream become a reality without accomplishing that thing God designed us for</u>.

Before I knew that I was earmarked for a predestined purpose, I thought that getting married, having kids, becoming wealthy and maintaining a powerful position was my ideal purpose. Being a housewife, caretaker, and mother are definitely a part of our purpose, and women have been earmarked to do that as well as other designated things.

I don't want to downplay the vitally significant role that housewives, mothers, and caretakers play and there may be seasons that you fulfill these roles and these alone. Also, we each have to seek God for the totality of what we were earmarked for. I, too am a mother, have been a full-time housewife and God revealed to me that He also earmarked me to be and do other things.

Prayer is the place where I get my instructions. God desires me to be a woman who is humble, worthy, and chosen to carry out the assignments and vision He reveals to me. I stay in a place of prayer and listening so I can be guided in every season of my life, embracing it day by day, week by week, month by month, and every year of life.

Purpose is accomplished daily in the little acts of love, such as sharing God's love with others in whatever opportunity God gives to us. For me, it includes raising my children, and pouring my life into others by sacrificially giving my money, time, and resources. Once upon a time, I thought material things such as a large home, luxury cars, expensive diamonds and furs— "a pretty girls dream" – were the epitome of a good life and that these things would bring me happiness. But I understand that my pretty dream and earmarked purpose is not to accumulate things and things can never bring me true joy, identity, nor purpose.

God has earmarked me not to blend into the culture and do what society or anyone else expects me to do. **He destined me to challenge and change the culture and do those things that He earmarked me to do as a delicate, compassionate, nurturing, and strong woman.** For me, it is simply helping those in need, writing books, sustaining my business, managing and overseeing my non-profit. Also, supporting missions in India, Africa, and Haiti and investing my life and monies in helping others fulfill their dreams in the kingdom.

You, like I, have a vision and earmarked purpose from God and your uniqueness, personality, proclivities, and specific make-up as a woman is needed to complete what God shows you. It is what you were handpicked and designated to fulfill – a specific purpose that only you can do. God set you apart to do this thing.

People are waiting on you and problems need your solutions. It will require you to take a leap of faith to launch into your earmarked purpose, but the more you spend introspective time with Him, the more He will reveal His plan to you and the better He can lead and guide you, step-by-step into doing and seeing your earmarked, pretty dream become a reality.

Journal Entry #3

1. What do you think it means to be earmarked?

   _____
   _____
   _____
   _____

2. What is your understanding of evil and how can forces try to stop us from fulfilling our earmarked purpose? How can you grow in your strength and power to defeat the dark forces?

   _____
   _____
   _____
   _____

3. Are you in an unhealthy relationship and do you need to break it off? Why? How and when do you plan to do that? Or is there a relationship from your past that was unhealthy for you? Why?

   _____
   _____
   _____
   _____

4. Do you believe in yourself and do you value the gift in you?

   _____

5. What is your purpose and identity apart from a man? What did God earmark you for and are you walking in it? Explain.

   _____
   _____
   _____
   _____

CHAPTER 4

Tenacious

No matter how many times we get knocked down, we get up! The words of Dr. Maya Angelou's poem, "And Still I Rise" best describe the prettiest, most tenacious spirit a woman can possess. And her verses quoted below say:

> You may write me down in history
> With your bitter, twisted lies,
> You may trod me in the very dirt
> But still, like dust, I'll rise.
>
> Does my sassiness upset you?
> Why are you beset with gloom?
> 'Cause I walk like I've got oil wells
> Pumping in my living room.
>
> Just like moons and like suns,
> With the certainty of tides,
> Just like hopes springing high,
> Still I'll rise.
>
> Did you want to see me broken?
> Bowed head and lowered eyes?
> Shoulders falling down like teardrops,
> Weakened by my soulful cries?
>
> Does my haughtiness offend you?
> Don't you take it awful hard
> 'Cause I laugh like I've got gold mines
> Diggin' in my own backyard.

You may shoot me with your words,
You may cut me with your eyes,
You may kill me with your hatefulness,
But still, like air, I'll rise.

Does my sexiness upset you?
Does it come as a surprise?
That I dance like I've got diamonds
At the meeting of my thighs?
Out of the huts of history's shame
I rise
Up from a past that's rooted in pain
I rise

    Maya Angelou knew something was inside of her and deep inside of us that causes women and even humankind to rise above the atrocities of life, and do it with *chutzpah,* a laugh, and some pep in our step. She, like I, understood that God built tenacity in all of us. It is that pretty spirit that is determined, persists, and is not easily discouraged.

    There is something about a tenacious woman. A tenacious woman has the ability to go through challenges, and **STILL RISE**, even after failed relationships, being traumatized, and rejected. She is able to endure the trials of life, but yet still rise out of the ashes of defeat, the ashes of pain, and the ashes of disappointment. There are too many things women have endured, suffered, and courageously overcome to note in the pages of this book, but I'd like to highlight a few women who provide an example of a tenacious spirit that is to be admired and emulated.

    In 2019, an awesome movie came to the big screen entitled ***Harriett.*** This movie told the story of a tenacious woman named Harriett Tubman who overcame insurmountable odds and the devastating circumstances of slavery to carry out the will of God in her life. Because she lived during the time of slavery, her life was in danger every time she made a decision to defy her master and help free others. Though she had no education, was unable to read maps and had no clear path to travel to her freedom, she had a unique ability to hear instruction and garner vision from God. She was tenacious because she knew God was going to lead and guide every action. She was so determined that she made several bold declarations and saw them become a reality right before her eyes.

I love the part in the movie where she's sitting on the ledge of the bridge, ready to jump into treacherous waters and she looked at her master and said, "Ain't going back. I want to be free. I will be dead or free." She was willing to die for her freedom and fortunately, God led her to freedom, but her tenacity did not stop there. Once she gained her freedom, she risked her life to help free others.

Tenacity means resolve, persistent, driven, and having an uncanny determination. Harriett possessed all of these character traits and more. God had deposited steadfastness within her and gave her the faith and tenacity as a woman warrior to do what had never been done before. She was determined that she was purposed to help seventy slaves cross over into freedom. She lost not one.

The P (purpose) and T (tenacity) in her pretty were definitely the aroma she radiated and women today are being influenced by her life's story. Thank goodness, it has prompted something in me and others to never give up, and to trust God beyond what we can see. It causes us to be determined to fulfill what God asks us, and have the fortitude to hear God and carry out His instructions, even if it may cost us our life. A daunting and unbelievable goal at best, but we can do all things through Christ, if we only believe like Harriett. Thank you, Harriett Tubman, for your example.

I'd like to highlight another tenacious woman who, against all odds, was also able to rise above her overwhelming circumstances and be healed after twelve years of physical, emotional and mental pain. This woman is infamous and unnamed in the Bible and, as a matter of fact, she is known by her issue rather than her name. But she is spoken of and discussed millions of times over, because of her great faith and her tenacious spirit to rise above her circumstances and continue to believe, endure ridicule and shame to find healing and wholeness from the only person who could truly erase her condition and ugliness and make her pretty again. Let's examine this story in greater depth.

> And a woman having an issue of blood twelve years, which had spent all her living upon physicians, neither could be healed of any, Came behind [him], and touched the border of his garment: and immediately her issue of blood stanched. And Jesus said, Who touched me? When all denied, Peter and they that were with him said, Master, the multitude throng thee and press [thee], and sayest thou, Who touched me? And Jesus said, Somebody hath touched me: for I perceive that virtue is gone out of me. And when the woman saw that she was not hid, she came trembling, and falling down before him, she declared unto him before all the people for what cause she had touched him, and how she was healed immediately. And he said unto her, Daughter, be of good comfort: thy faith hath made thee whole; go in peace (Luke 8:43-50 KJV).

As we closely examine this woman's story, we note that this woman's tenacity is what allowed her to be made whole and granted her a healing miracle. First, she had this issue for twelve years. Truthfully, how many of us would have given up after year five or six? This was a hemorrhaging that she suffered from not five, six, or seven years, but twelve. It was her tenacious pursuit to be healed that caused her to spend probably thousands of dollars until she exhausted all of her funds on doctors to find a cure, but her condition got even worse.

At this point, many would get mad with God. We could accuse Him of putting this issue on us. But not this woman. She did quite the opposite, because she had a relentless spirit that chased after God instead of turning away from Him. She knew she had exhausted all of her strength and financial resources to find healing, so she pressed her way to Jesus. She knew she had to press past her shame, pride, and her issue to find Jesus, because He could do for her what no one else could.

Tenacity and faith stood up in her and she pressed through the crowd, through her embarrassment, and determined that she was going to get her touch and freedom that day, no matter what it took. And because of her tenacious spirit, she was healed and made whole immediately. Her ugly became her pretty.

I can relate to both Harriett and this woman with an issue of blood. I wouldn't equate myself to women of such caliber, but I know too well what it looks like to be tenacious and find strength to rise above the unexpected pains of life. As women, God put a second wind in us, and we will find a way out of no way. We will make a meal out of a few items in the cupboard, and we will bounce back after severe devastation and pain. I kept bouncing back adversity after adversity. The tenacity in me would not give up and I'd like to attribute my bounce back attitude to being a female athlete. There's something in a woman's DNA that allows us to keep going and show up in the game, even when we're in pain.

In my early days in ministry, I was a stallion, both anxious and quick to fulfill God's vision. But God tested my tenacity and commitment and eventually I ran out of gas. I remember planting and pastoring our first church. I was so rambunctious and energetic. Then came the rejection, pain, and long years of what I termed failure. There were times I was disappointed by those whom I loved, and I felt so dejected, unappreciated, and under-equipped that I wanted to quit.

As a young woman, I spoke with boldness, and I often confronted injustice and challenged unhealthy practices or inequitable systems. Consequently, there were times I received backlash as a result of being bold. This backlash came in several ways. Sometimes people rejected me. And other times, people distanced themselves from me, dissolved our relationship, or disappeared. These hurtful occurrences began to rattle my confidence and shake my resolve.

Things worsened after I gathered my strength in a third attempt to bring to life a sinking ministry by merging with a more stable leader who could guide us, lend resources, and collaborate with us to help our dream be sustained. However, it was a merger that didn't work, but rather extinguished my vision and quenched my creative flow. The leader rejected many of my ideas, excluded me, and my strong personality as a leader of my non-profit (Blossoming Vines, Inc.) was not welcomed. This rejection diminished my zeal and tenacity for ministry.

I began to withdraw from some and felt intimidated by others. I became passive and paranoid about everything. Intimidation had taken root in my heart and I lost my confidence and the **P and R in my** pretty. No longer did I feel **purposeful** and I did not feel **received** or accepted. I entered a state of depression and spiraled into an abyss of self-loathing, rebellion, and worldly gratifications to ease the pain and forget the hurt.

I tried everything in my strength to bounce back, but the tenacious Sonia finally reached a place of depletion. Just like the woman with the issue of blood, I tried everything, and exhausted all of my ideas, energy, and tears. I needed God to do for me what I could not do for myself. I needed His touch to help me come out of darkness and give me passion and purpose again.

When I finally had no more strength or tenacity, God came in and rescued me. He gave me a rope and pulled me out of the abyss and begin to nourish me back to health. I had a little hope, mustard-seed faith, and a glimmer of a vision that kept me holding on and forging forward through the pain. During this process, God was humbling me, settling past issues, and teaching me to love, no matter how people treated me.

Also, He was dealing with my insecurities, pride, and desire for control. He humbled me and taught me that my strength was not in my ability to pull myself up, but it was in relenting and realizing that I needed Him to fight my battles. **Though I am tenacious, I now realize my tenacity, my** pretty **and my strength are empowered by Him.**

How many times have others rejected you, but you bounced back in the midst of adversity and major challenges? How many times have you made a way out of no way and pressed your way to continue to survive because so many people are depending on you? Though you are tired mentally, physically, and spiritually, you just keep going because the tenacity in you will not let you quit.

Even as you're reading these words, tears are rolling down your cheeks and a big lump is in your throat, because you're at your wits end and you really don't have the strength to go any further. This is the point that God desires for you to relent and admit that you can't do it anymore. Cry out to Him that you need Him to do for you what you can't do for yourself!

A **tenacious spirit** is one that is surrendered to Him which **gives you the strength and boldness to rise above it all and become everything that He desires you to be**!

Journal Entry #4

1. Do you have a tenacious spirit? If so, please describe it. If not, why not?

   _____
   _____
   _____
   _____

2. What two women can you describe as tenacious? Name a woman from history or who is currently living and a Biblical woman. Why do you feel each is tenacious?

   _____
   _____
   _____
   _____

3. Has anything happened in your life that sucked the life out of you? What was it?

   _____
   _____
   _____
   _____

4. Describe where you are mentally and spiritually since that happened.

   _____
   _____
   _____
   _____

5. A tenacious spirit is one that is **surrendered** to Him and gives you the boldness, strength, and a **path of healing** to become all that He desires you to be! Are you surrendered to God? Why or why not? What is your path to healing?

_____
_____
_____
_____

After answering these questions, you may realize you're still struggling in areas, as we all are and need a defined path to healing and wholeness. My prayer is that this book is helping to kindle some healing in your heart and direct you to areas that need your attention.

However, the path to healing is different for each of us. Some may need maintenance and some of you may be embarking on an intense and deep journey to healing. It may require some efforts that I've mentioned before such as therapy, prayer, an accountability partner, getting off of social media, and daily walking out our process with prayer and study of His Word.

As you answer question number five in your journal entry, be very specific and seek God and godly counsel regarding the best path for you and be willing to *commit to the work* until you see and feel some progress. Your confidence will be restored and the T (tenacious) in your pretty will be even more fortified and powerful **as you do the work and surrender to Him**.

CHAPTER 5

*T*riumphant

A triumphant life is one full of victory and success that is exciting, exhilarating, and breathes life into others. It is one where we have overcome most of the challenges and trials of our life and found purpose in our pain. Triumphant living is swaggering in such a way that what the enemy meant for evil, you can brag and say, "**God turned it around for good**." Your triumphant life influences other's lives, and you can see your defeats as victories and stepping stones to a greater purpose. A few years ago, a popular song by Vashawn Mitchell spoke of a triumphant life where the battle was won and the song emphasized the fact that a greater power is in us.

If the battle is already won, then why is triumphant, victorious and celebratory living by-passing so many? Why does winning seem so foreign? When we are used to losing or holding our breath until the next mishap in life occurs, it's hard to visualize and believe we can have a triumphant life.

Ironically, a triumphant and victorious life is what many display on Instagram and Facebook. Filtered pictures of ravishing outfits, flawless faces and tapered bodies are posted on the regular. Relationships are glorified and husbands and wives seem so happy and in love. We smile for the camera and show most of the positive highlights of our life and encourage people to believe that our life is superb and we are living a triumphant life. But in reality, if the truth be told, many of our marriages are hanging on by a thread, we dislike our job, our children are causing us unrest, and we're living paycheck to paycheck.

We rarely like what we see in the mirror. We really don't feel pretty, even though we pretend to have it all together. We are hurting on the inside and what we project on social media is not what is really happening in our hearts.

Granted, not everyone is pretending and some of us are living triumphantly or moving in that direction. However, Matthew 7:14 says, "Because narrow [is] the gate and difficult [is] the way which leads to life, and **there are few who find it**." This tells us that very few people find a triumphant life, but rather find an empty life or materialistic life, void of true purpose.

Why does this Scripture imply that very few people find a triumphant life? I believe very few people find it because it is narrow and difficult. I suggest that it is narrow and difficult, because it requires us to *uncover deep rooted issues in our life*, *let go of our selfish dreams*, and finally *it takes walking in faith and humility,* every step of our life's journey.

A triumphant life is attainable and pretty girls – yes pretty women – can have this victorious life, but in order for our pretty to become triumphant, it must get uglier first. I know I've had you dig deep, but let's dig a little deeper and know that greater triumphant living is possible. You're not far from it, if you're not already walking in it.

Most of us have heard the cliché, "a diamond in the rough." And most of us have rough edges and ugly things in our lives and in our hearts that need chiseling and excavating. The diamond never shines until it goes through an arduous process – extraction, crushing, and refining.

Self-examination is not always an easy thing. Many times, **we may find it difficult to acknowledge the ugly in our heart**, but we must be truthful with ourselves and with God. We all have rough edges and the sooner we expose them, the quicker God can remove them and heal us. **He can't heal what we hide.**

The moment I was confronted with this truth, I was not so eager to acknowledge my ugly as I began to see it show up in my life in so many ways and I was tired of seeing and dealing with it. My pride, lust, judgmental spirit, and my need for control were the issues God exposed first.

I remember when I surrendered my heart to God, I was sitting in church, lusting after a handsome preacher in the pulpit. I was thinking of ways I could get his attention and seduce him. I was so ashamed, wondering why in the world was I lusting after this man when I was trying to live a life of purity. God was allowing these lustful thoughts to arise so I could acknowledge them and He could help me get free from them.

I had to admit that I was having sexual thoughts for this man, and I prayed and asked God to free me from them and help me to have pure and righteous thoughts. I did not realize my past promiscuous life, provocative dressing, clubbing, and using my body to garner attention from men would follow me, but unfortunately lust did trail me. It was still showing up until God helped me get free. With prayer and therapy, God's grace, love, and power liberated me from these lustful thoughts, and I begin to look at men in a healthy way.

Next, I had to deal with that **ugly spirit of pride**. Pride can show up in a number of different ways in our lives. Pride can be arrogance, conceit, self-importance, or an egotistical attitude. It can also cause you to turn down help when you need it, or fail to acknowledge that you're broken and in need of healing. This type of denial is pride cloaked in humility, but it's just a smoke screen, inhibiting us from telling the truth.

My pride was obvious, because I thought I was better than others and was very vain and arrogant. I felt because I had a bachelor's and master's degree and was successful in most things, ministry success would come easy to me and I would be known across platforms and seen before crowds. Because I was pretty on the outside, vanity caused me to put my aesthetics above most things. As I said earlier, it was my trump card. I used my looks to get into places, date professional athletes, and pump my confidence and ego. This attitude was faulty and self-willed at its core.

Though the world pushes us to be ambitious, overconfident, and use our physical attributes to get ahead in life, God espouses another way which requires humility and internal character. Thus, God had to free me from pride. His method allowed many disappointments, failures, and rejections to happen in my life to bring my prideful issue to my attention. **God will allow disappointments and unfair things to happen in our life to get our attention**. We can either get angry at God about certain situations or we can investigate what lesson God wants us to learn from the disappointment or unfair trial in our life.

If you can identify and had to list what failures, disappointments or unfair things have happened in your life, what would you write? **My failures helped me see my arrogance and humbled me to recognize my ugly conceit**. I soon learned that no degree, pedigree, intelligence, looks or athletic ability could earn me status or success in life. When I admitted my pride, God enabled me with the ability to succeed. And true successful and triumphant living came as I humbled myself and begin to do things His way to fulfill my God-given purpose in the earth.

You too are a diamond in the rough and there are issues in your heart that God desires to free you from. Acknowledging and admitting those areas in prayer is the first step to freedom. Pride, lust, and control were areas I confessed, and you may also see these in your heart. You may also notice your issues show up as an ugly attitude and language, jealousy, fear, manipulation, or gossip.

Most of us know what our issues are, and it doesn't take rocket science to figure them out, but it does take courage to come clean and be willing to go through a process of being freed from them. Sometimes, this process may take longer than others and it may require you to get to the root of why you behave or think in unhealthy ways.

Fortunately, God gives us a recipe for healing and wholeness and **when we follow that recipe, we become better people and better people can live better lives**. Not only better lives, but

triumphant lives. Remember, if you'd like your diamond to shine, then extraction, crushing, and refining is most necessary. After the cutting and refining of some of your issues, you will shine. This chapter's journal entry will highlight a few other tools and processes that may be helpful in uncovering root issues, but let's keep digging right now.

Triumphant living also requires us letting go of our preconceived and planned lives and laying hold of the life God has planned for us. Most of us have a vision and a plan of what we desire to fulfill in life and have some idea of what we want to become. We've seen it, thought about it, and many of us have planned it out. We may spend the majority of our life preparing for this plan and aggressively pursuing it. But Proverbs 19:21 tells us, "**Many are the plans in a person's heart, but it is the LORD's purpose that prevails.**" This is why I alluded to the fact that triumphant living can be difficult and few find it, because it requires letting go of our plans and this can be hard.

Matthew 10:39 says, "Whoever finds their life will lose it, and whoever loses their life for my sake will find it. It may be hard to lose your life, give up your plans, and turn from your selfish ambitions. Though it may be difficult to embrace the challenges of life, and whole-heartedly follow God, the rewards definitely outweigh the challenges when you relent to God's way.

Another key to living a triumphant life is understanding what losing our life actually means, Let's apprehend this key before ending this chapter.

Losing your life may seem drastic if we view it literally, but losing your life is being willing to lay down the plan you had for yourself. When I graduated from college, I planned to move to California, launch a successful modeling and sports journalism career and marry a professional athlete. I had it all mapped out. I was aggressively pursuing this path and had a modeling portfolio and was dating a professional football player who played for the San Francisco 49ers. He was my ticket to the life I had envisioned.

Fortunately, after baby mama drama with my boyfriend and countless nights of experiencing heartache and pain regarding my empty life and superficial, selfish dreams, I asked God for an encounter with Him for real. And on May 22, 1992, God answered my prayer and I experienced Him in a real way. At that moment, my heart was no longer the same and my desires begin to change.

I broke up with my boyfriend and promised God that I would pursue Him, stop fornicating, and wait until marriage. I had an insatiable hunger to read the Bible and learn more about God. My encounter with God occurred at twenty-two years of age and that was the point my life began to change for the better. It was also the point I gained an authentic purpose for my life. He asked me to lay down the dream I had dreamt and to pick up the life He had for me.

I was young and energetic, so I was more than willing, though I didn't know the sacrifices, challenges, and path it would take me on, but one thing that I did know is that His life for me would reap eternal rewards and had more sustenance than the life I'd previously chosen.

Whose life are you living? Is it the life God planned for you? Are you willing to lay down your life in order to find His perfect will for you? These are the questions you must answer in order to consider His plan for your life. Making the necessary sacrifices, enduring challenges, and experiencing unplanned things gives us the opportunity to impact others' lives in a greater way.

Let His dreams become your dreams and endeavor to hear what His plan is by listening and getting impressions. If this sounds like a broken recorded, it's because I am reiterating the same principles and concepts. No the record isn't broken. Pretty requires us to get these godly principles and rethink them over and over again until we apply them in our life.

Do you know the plan and purpose God has for you? Providentially, God does. Jeremiah 29:11 says, **"For I know the plans I have for you, says the LORD. They are plans for good and not for disaster, to give you a future and a hope."** His triumphant plans have so much hope and promise, if we are willing to trust Him and follow His leading.

Things will not always be crystal clear and there will times we may doubt, but if we trust Him and step line-by-line, He will gently guide us back onto the right path, if we happen to veer off. Do you feel valued and loved by God? Does your life matter? Are you able to relent to the work to become a healed and whole individual? Can you lay down your plans, learn His plan for your life, and follow Him without reservations and excuses?

If you are able, spring forward and continue this journey called life. **Though it will not be perfect, triumphant living will be your portion**. Your pretty life will have value and most importantly, it will be a gateway for others to live a victorious and triumphant life also.

Here's the conundrum – just as He gave His life that we might live a glorious and meaningful life, we too must give up our life, though not literally, for others to live and for the world to become a better place.

I'd like to share a friend's story to illustrate another example of what it means to give up your life. This woman's story is so inspiring because she is the archetype of a person who gave up her plan to fulfill the plan of God for her life. She went through medical school, completed her residency and became a medical doctor but at some juncture, God revealed to her the next phase of His plan for her life. He asked her to leave her medical profession and become a missionary in Africa.

So my friend Sherri quit her practice and began to prepare to follow the plan God had shown her. With excitement and probably some uncertainty, she moved to a small town in Cameroon in West Africa and started a school of ministry with the help of family and friends in America. She embarked on a life that was foreign to her – a life that didn't have the comforts of a physician's salary and a life that required her to give her time, money, and talent to people she didn't know in a place that was thousands of miles from her home.

It took courage, faith, and tenacity to boldly step out and follow the path God had planned for her. And to this date, she has impacted many lives, raised up many students and changed the trajectory of people and made an impact in the continent of Africa that will continue to reverberate in the lives of others as she fulfills her purpose.

Her pretty aroma has even touched my life as I too was impacted by her life's work when I was able to visit her newest school in Nairobi, Kenya. She is living a victorious, glorious, and triumphant life, because she chose to lay down her plan and follow His plan.

Maybe God is not asking you to leave your profession and move to Africa. Or maybe He's not asking to you to give up modeling or sports journalism and enter the ministry. Maybe your profession is your purpose, or maybe you are called to start a business, build a transitional home, support missions, preach the gospel, or something else that God is specifically showing and tugging on your heart to do.

If it's a plan that seems too big, too far-fetched, and beyond your capacity, it's probably God. As you spend time with the Him, He will release the "what" and the "how" to you if He has not done so already. Will the release be spot on? No, it will require you to walk by faith and not by sight, but He will continue to guide you every step of the way.

Like both Sherri and I, be courageous, bold and tenacious enough to march or continue marching towards your triumphant life. Remember, miracles don't happen if you stay in the boat. They happen when you get out of the boat and start walking. You'll find yourself walking on water just like Peter, but he had to get out of the boat. And guess what? Unlike Peter, as a woman, you 'll be walking on water pretty and gracefully, as you catwalk the runway of your life. **Your pretty triumphant life awaits you, so let's journey onward!**

Journal Entry #5

1. Name a few issues that you know are in your heart (such as lust, pride, anger, resentment, self-loathing). What root causes can these issues be attributed to?

   _____
   _____
   _____
   _____

2. Does your life matter? Why?

   _____
   _____

3. Are you willing to work relentlessly to become a healed and whole individual?

   _____
   _____
   _____
   _____

4. Can you lay down your plans, learn His plan for you, and can you follow Him without reservations and excuses?

   _____
   _____
   _____
   _____

5. What does a triumphant life look like to you?

   _____
   _____
   _____
   _____

CHAPTER 6

Yielded to Yield

     This last chapter is the culmination of all of the other chapters, because in order to walk in purpose, be received, know that you're earmarked, be tenacious, and live triumphantly, you must be fully yielded to the Father, which allows you to yield fruit. Basically, **yielding is releasing your own strength and surrendering to His power and following His plan to success**.

     Chapter 5 helped us surrender our selfish plans and navigate towards the plans of God. Here, I am emphasizing yielding as a two-fold concept which includes yielding to the Father so that we can yield and generate more fruit in God's kingdom. God does not make an investment in our life without expecting us to yield results. His fruit includes the lives we touch, change and help bring into the kingdom of God.

     His ultimate purpose is to rescue and change us so we can likewise reach and help others get rescued and so they can change their lives as well. In other words, He does not clarify our purpose, affirm our worthiness, earmark our destiny, build our tenacity, or give us a triumphant life without expecting us to yield (produce) results.

     Mark 8 tells a parable about a sower who sows seeds in different types of soils and how the right soil will yield crops that bring increase.

> Then He taught them many things by parables, and said to them in His teaching: "Listen! Behold, a sower went out to sow. And it happened, as he sowed, [that] some [seed] fell by the wayside; and

the birds of the air came and devoured it. Some fell on stony ground, where it did not have much earth; and immediately it sprang up because it had no depth of earth. But when the sun was up it was scorched, and because it had no root it withered away. And some [seed] fell among thorns; and the thorns grew up and choked it, and it yielded no crop. But other [seed] fell on good ground and yielded a crop that sprang up, increased and produced: some thirtyfold, some sixty, and some a hundred" (Mark 4:2-8 NKJV).

A parable is a story told in the culture and time of the storyteller to accentuate a point that can be understood by those who hear it. This parable uses the metaphor of farming, which was very relatable in that time period. In Biblical times, everyone planted and harvested food. However, we too can relate to this parable because most of us understand the analogy of sowing, planting, and reaping.

The analogy delineates the sower as God and our heart as the soil. Crops refer to the people whose lives are changed and eternally shifted as a result of the seed that is sown in us, so that we can reproduce it in others. If our heart is stony or thorny, it will not yield crops. Meaning, in order for us to produce results, we must open our heart and allow God to plant His Word in it. **His Word will cause us to walk in our earmarked purpose and produce pretty fruit.** When the word falls in a pretty heart, it yields a crop, increases and produces 30, 60, and some 100.

The more we surrender to the Father, the more results we can return to Him. The principle of yielding and duplication is actualized in our life when we abide in the Father, which means **to stay in His presence, remain in His will**, and **allow Him to guide and lead our life**. When you abide in God, not only do you achieve a fruitful life, but when He sees your fruitfulness, He uses you all the more to generate even more in His kingdom.

<u>Abiding requires being intentional and laying aside distractions to assure you spend quality and consistent time with God</u>. It means being aware of God's presence at all times and following His path. When we abide in Him, it is definitely worth the favorable results. Let's delve into John 15:1-4 to further grasp yielding.

> I am the true vine, and My Father is the vinedresser. Every branch in Me that does not bear fruit He takes away; and every [branch] that bears fruit He prunes, that it may bear more fruit. You are already clean because of the word which I have spoken to you. Abide in Me, and I in you. As the branch cannot bear fruit of itself, unless it abides in the vine, neither can you, unless you abide in Me (John 15:1-4, NKJV).

This Scripture reminds us that we cannot produce anything apart from Him. We must be strengthened and nourished by Him as we walk in His purpose. Abiding compels us to stay connected to God in a consistent and authentic relationship with Him. It involves many of the things we've discussed in this book such as praying to hear our purpose, identifying places in our life that need healing, and giving up our plan to accept and follow His plan, to reiterate a few.

Abiding doesn't mean you'll have a perfect relationship with God, but one that continues to grow and develop. If we abide in Him, He will use us to produce more fruit. If He sees you doing well, He will prune you to do even better. Pruning is also a term used by gardeners. It literally means cutting away dead or overgrown branches, especially to increase fruitfulness and growth. This metaphorically means that if there is anything dead or overgrown, God will cut it out of your life so He can increase your fruitfulness.

I have experienced being pruned and wasn't aware that this was what I was going through, as it was very painful, uncomfortable, and lonely. I told you I was a young twenty-two year-old, enthusiastic girl, running for Jesus. I was so eager to please God that I was sharing His Word with any and everybody, without any inhibitions or fear.

I entered inner-city ministry and went to impoverished communities to mentor young girls. I entered ministry training at twenty-four and studied theology to better prepare for my purpose as a minister and pastor. I studied at Oral Roberts University, and knew my purpose was to be His mouthpiece.

After graduate school, my hubby and I planted our first church and saw many come to Christ. Then, we relaunched our church a few years later and sowed seed and saw fruit produced in that church. During that time, I launched my non-profit, women's ministry called Blossoming Vines Ministries and held countless prayer gatherings, evangelistic outreaches, and served single moms and young girls. Stick with me, I am proving a point as I outline my past fruitful works. In 2015, we merged our church and became campus pastors of our third church while still supporting our church in Haiti and supporting missions in both India and Africa. I felt we were well on our way; the fruit we were producing was increasing and success seemed imminent. However, right in the middle of our growth, I was given an ultimatum to walk away from leading my non-profit, if we desired to continue as campus pastors. We decided to step down as campus pastors, because both my hubby and I believed it was our time to sit down from pastoring and for me to continue leading Blossoming Vines. What I thought was ascending to my most fruitful life, spiraled into rejection and termination.

I was devastated and did not understand why God was putting a halt to the His plan for my life. I had to stop running so fast for Jesus and be pruned so God could produce more fruit from my life. Pruning meant **He interrupted the plan, allowed me to suffer rejection**, and **forced me to see other areas in my life that needed healing**. He needed to cut away dead and overgrown things in my life in order to increase my fruitfulness. This process was not easy, but necessary. And after all the things I'd endured, one would think I'd had enough. However, the process of transformation is ongoing and every pruning season always produces pretty results.

Pruning was a three-year process of seclusion in a foreign place where I was no longer doing the thing I was most passionate about. The vision I thought was coming to fruition died right before my eyes. I became disoriented, discouraged, and void of purpose. I didn't even know if I was called to do what God has shown me to do.

I spent most nights laying in a bed of depression, drinking my cares away, and waddling in self-pity. I stopped attending church and stopped reading His word regularly. I was going through the motions and hurting severely on the inside. My confidence had faded, my joy was gone, and my tenacity was depleted. I sat in my pity party and was waiting on God to vindicate me and lift me to a mountain top experience.

Instead, He allowed me to waddle in self-pity until I got sick and tired of my depressive situation, and began to cry out to God to free me and heal my broken, disappointed heart. Subsequently, God begin to heal my heart and help me recover my courage, strength, and desire to move forward in my life.

As I yielded to the pruning season, God cut my prideful ways, eradicated my self-loathing, and taught me that my self-worth was not in what I did, but it was in Him and Him alone. It was a slow process of healing, but I kept stepping towards healing and wholeness.

Little by little, day by day, I felt myself getting stronger and stronger. I learned to forgive those who hurt me and let go of the resentful feelings I'd carried. I began to renew my fervor for God and gained new insight and vision regarding the next phase of my purpose. I began to see like never before that everything I had lost and the failure and rejection I'd experienced were all a part of God's plan to teach me to trust Him wholeheartedly.

I also began to realize my self-worth was not in my performing, and that He uniquely created me **with distinct peculiarities**, **a prophetic edge**, **compassionate heart**, and a

boldness to speak up for others. I began to unapologetically love everything about me and realized I was being prepared to do an even greater work and produce triple the fruit I had produced in the past.

My yielded spirit is enabling me to yield more for God. This season of my life is the prettiest it's ever been. I am no longer bound by the constraints of men, but I am free to follow God's purpose by yielding to Him continuously. The best is yet to come and the vision is greater than I could have thought or imagined. That which He had me walk away from and give up was just the catalyst to the greater vision He desires me to fulfill in the earth.

As you yield to the Father, He desires you also to produce greater fruit. Every trial, disappointment, rejection, and failure, is all a set up for your comeback. Only you know exactly where you are in this season of your life, so be patient with yourself and with God. He is **pruning you and causing you to yield to His process so you can yield more fruit in His Kingdom**. This process may take time, and will require God to cut away those things in your life and heart that prevent you from producing more for Him.

It may be time to forgive someone in your life that deeply hurt you. Also, this is a season where you can let go of rejection and self-deprecation and begin to love all of the "pretty you" that God created. As you surrender daily, He will expose things in you in order to cut them out of your heart, so nothing will regretfully inhibit you from following His purpose.

You may be in a space you never foresaw and your dream has fizzled. Maybe you've lost a loved-one, divorced or are going through a divorce, got laid off from a job, don't see any ministry or opportunities opening up and this is causing you pain.

Maybe God is requiring you to yield to Him and rest during this season. It's okay to take the needed time by yourself **to refocus**, **reset**, and **heal**. Allow this time to get new vision, get stronger, gain your tenacity, and learn to love all of you – not just the external frame, but the inner you. The you that is rare, spectacular, gifted, and the original person God created you to be. You are His masterpiece. As this book nears its close, I'd like to share a poetical piece that I wrote after I learned **to love all of myself** and **realized I was His masterpiece**.

His Masterpiece

Be audacious
I am fearfully and wonderfully made,
Created from the tapestry of a Sovereign Father who has as many
Flavors, colors, sizes, tones—
Voice patterns, dialects as the fish of the sea;
I know this because He created me!

With my pretty light skin, kinky/fine hair whose texture is layered with many ripples, dips, patterns and shades that I choose to cover with a versatile easier way to maintain my mane not because I don't like my hair.

Yes, I love my hair which He knows every strand
And although you rarely see it—
I choose this head covering, because it's just convenient!

So you see, I've learned to love myself, yes all of my pretty self!
Though rejection, speculation and misjudgment happens every day,
because I'm bold, black, prophetic and speak truth when He asks me to say!

I am His mouthpiece, His voice, His vessel in the earth;
so don't box me in, nor create an image of what you'd like me to be.
It's through my journeys, trials, process, and tears
I've recompensed to be me!
Really, who else could I be?

So I asked you the same question as I change the direction in this rhythmic dialogue of words and expressions painted on this canvas of His masterpiece!

Yes, you pretty one- His Masterpiece
Created in His image and His likeness specifically carved, hand woven, hand chosen—
From your genealogy to your hue, size, shape, to indentions in your eye, dimples in your cheeks and even the tone and voice in which you speak!

His Masterpiece— that's why He put you on the potter's wheel
To fine tune you, pull that diamond from the rough while He spins and makes us and gets all that stuff.

That stuff that doesn't belong that's not Him but us—
So relent!
Let Him complete what He started
Certain things He want assent-- so don't you assent or dare to accept!

Do you believe and perceive that you are His masterpiece?

I am His masterpiece made to glorify Him with all my uniqueness and differences,
which clarify, define and authenticate who I be!
It's through my journeys, trials, process, and tears
I've recompensed to be me!
Really, who else could I be?

It's your uniqueness's and differences that quantify and qualify you—
Your journey, trials, process, and tears is what brought you through.

Recompense to, but better yet Sashay and Resolve to be you;
Really who else could do-- or be you!

Pretty one— His Masterpiece!

You are loved not because of what you do or how you look, but you are loved because **He deems you worthy and loves the masterpiece He created**. Yield to the Father so you can yield more for the Father. This world needs you as a whole, better, healed and *prettier* **version of you**. This *pretty* version of you is the woman who is *Purposed, Received, Earmarked, Tenacious, Triumphant, and Yielded*. This *pretty* **woman** is unstoppable, a world changer and a woman like the Proverbs 31 Woman.

> Who can find a virtuous wife? For her worth [is] far above rubies. The heart of her husband safely trusts her; So he will have no lack of gain. She does him good and not evil All the days of her life. ... She considers a field and buys it; From her profits she plants a vineyard. She girds herself with strength, And strengthens her arms. ... She extends her hand to the poor, Yes, she reaches out her hands to the needy. ... Strength and honor [are] her clothing; She shall rejoice in time to come. She opens her mouth with wisdom, And on her tongue [is] the law of kindness. She watches over the ways of her household, And does not eat the bread of idleness. Her children rise up and call her blessed; Her husband [also], and he praises her: "Many daughters have done well, But you excel them all." (Proverbs 31:10-12, 16-17, 20, 25-29, NKJV)

You are that *pretty* woman who does good and not evil, does business as God leads, has inner strength, extends your hands to the poor, and wisdom flows from your mouth. Honor and strength are your attire and not just the latest fashion trend, but you're fly too. Your tongue is kind, idleness does not consume you and your children (natural or other) call you blessed. You are excelling in this life and you are needed in His kingdom.

Even if you can't completely see this version of you right now, this is the woman God sees. And as you continue to yield to Him and His purpose—you will see this pretty picture become a reality in your life.

Say it with me again. I am Pretty! Purposed, Received, Earmarked, Tenacious, Triumphant, and Yielded!

Journal Entry #6

1. How do you yield to the Father?

   _____
   _____
   _____
   _____

2. List the fruit that you believe you are producing in the kingdom.

   _____
   _____
   _____
   _____

3. How are you abiding in God and what does that look like to you?

   _____
   _____
   _____
   _____

4. Is God pruning you? Explain what that process looks like in your life.

   _____
   _____
   _____
   _____

5. What qualities of the Proverbs 31 woman do you see in you? Read that Scripture again and write out those qualities.

   _____
   _____
   _____
   _____

6. What does being pretty mean to you? Do you think you're pretty? Why?

Final Thoughts

I pray this book has touched and changed your life in some way. My hope is that groups of women will start an, "I Am Pretty" reading club and study and discuss the principles, stories, and concepts discussed in this book.

Read chapters collaboratively with your sister friend(s) or best friend and then discuss the book as well as the journal questions. Complete all of the journal entries and meditate on the Scriptures outlined in each chapter and use them as your devotions.

In doing the work, if it **requires getting therapy, seeking healing and deliverance prayer, ramping up your devotional life**, letting go of unhealthy relationships and behavior, and **courageously doing things you've never done before- DO IT!**

Change doesn't come because we read the word, but it happens because we put the word into action and do the work, apply the principles, and relent to God's process. I no longer see my pretty as external but I have grasped the reality that I am PRETTY because I walk in my Purpose, am Received by the Father, am Earmarked for a specific plan, am Tenacious as He imparts my fervor and strength, live a Triumphant life, and continue to Yield to the Father daily as I yield more fruit in His Kingdom.

The next chapter in my book is yet to be written, but I am turning the page and promenading into the next part of my story as the pretty woman God created me to be. Come, let's take this journey together and create the next pretty story, so other women can be empowered also.